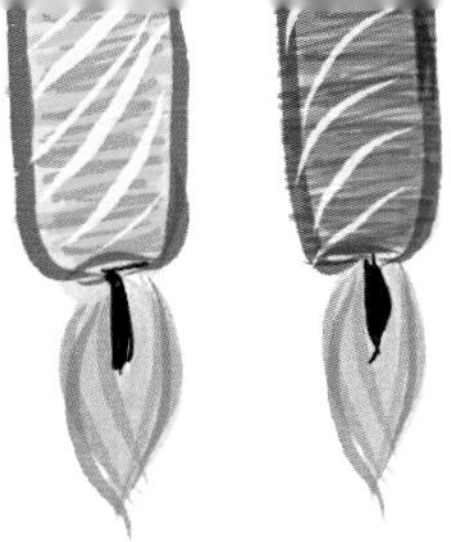

STOP and Read This Book

Words and Pictures
by Amanda Silva

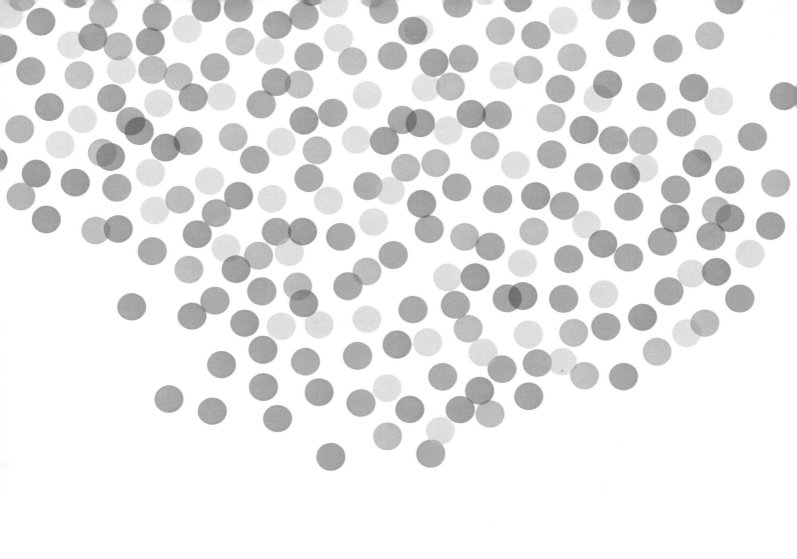

Published 2021 by the Book Badger LLC

Hello.

Are you ready for some

FUN?

Okay.

Let's Go!

Let's see...

Can you

BLOW

these candles out?

Oooh!

you got ONE.

let's try again.

That's

TWO.

Try for Three.

Hooray!

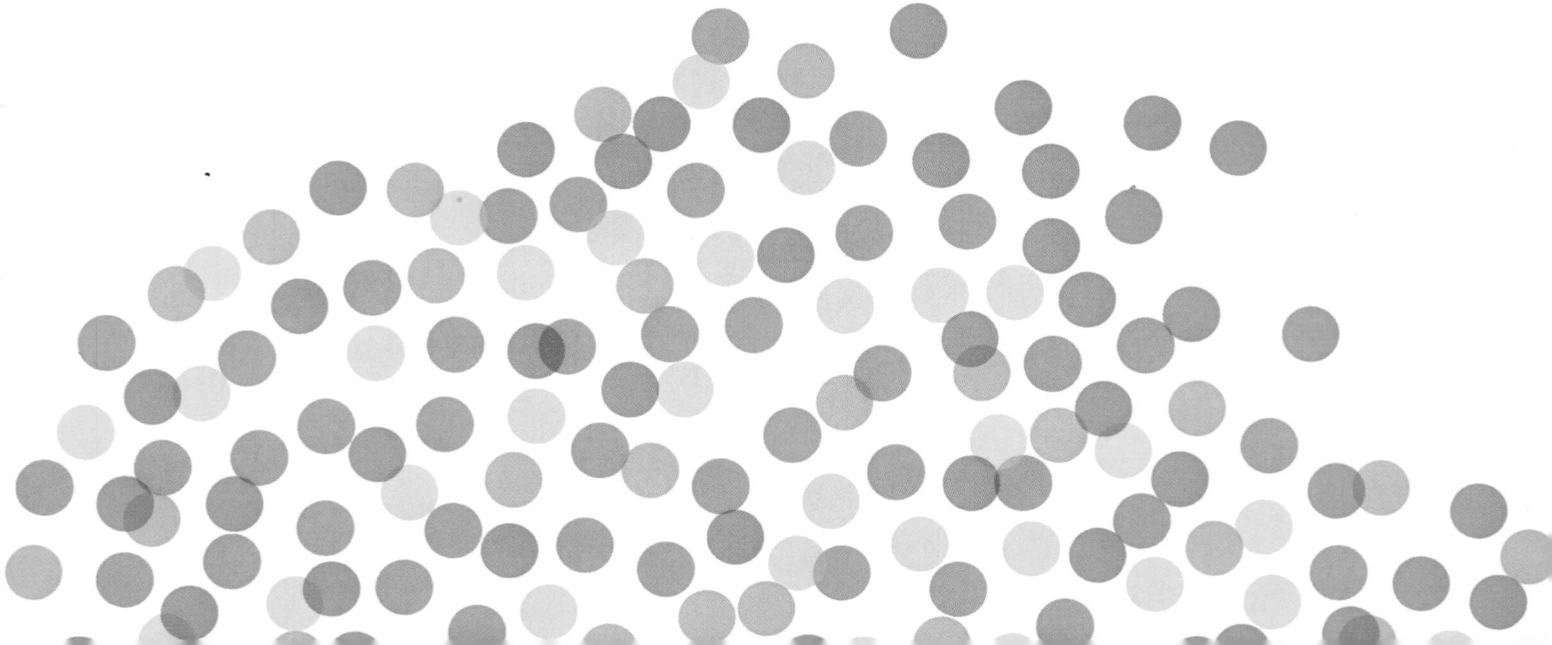

let's find something else to do...

this way -->

I think I lost a
strawberry
somewhere in these slices of
Watermelon
can you help me
Find it?

my friend

Ducky

likes to play

Hide

and

SEEK

Have you seen him?

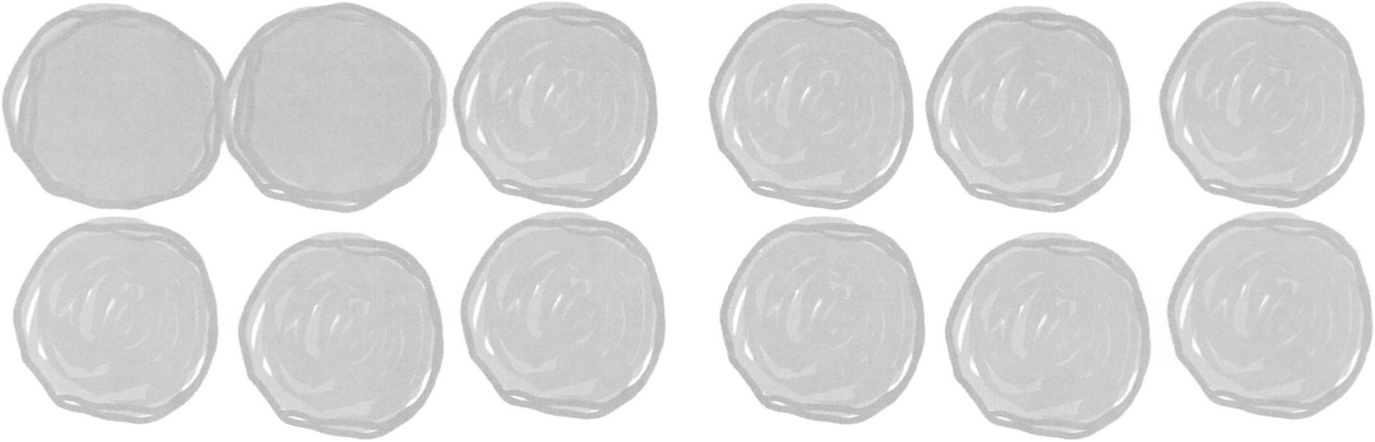

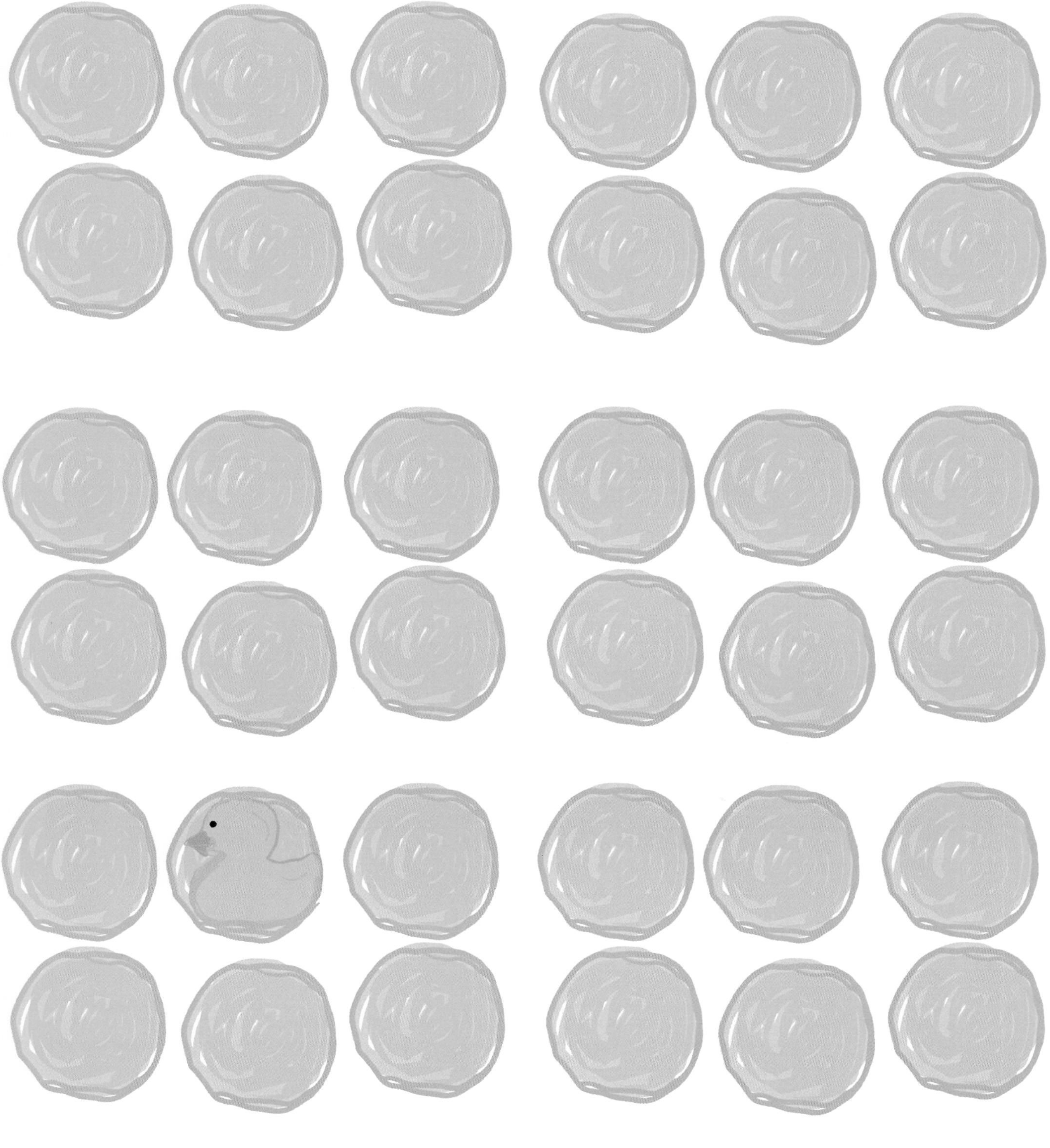

UNITED STATES OF AMERICA
ONE CENT
UNITED STATES OF AMERICA
ONE CENT
UNITED STATES OF AMERICA
ONE CENT
UNITED STATES OF AMERICA
ONE CENT

one of these pennies is

UNITED STATES OF AMERICA
ONE CENT
UNITED STATES OF AMERICA
ONE CENT
UNITED STATES OF AMERICA
ONE CENT
UNITED STATES OF AMERICA
ONE CENT
IN GOD WE TRUST
LIBERTY
1983
UNITED STATES OF AMERICA
ONE CENT
UNITED STATES OF AMERICA
ONE CENT
UNITED STATES OF AMERICA
ONE CENT

LUCKY.
can you guess which one?

sometimes you just have to

STOP and enjoy

the flowers

Is there one that makes you smile?

Follow this **path** with your finger.

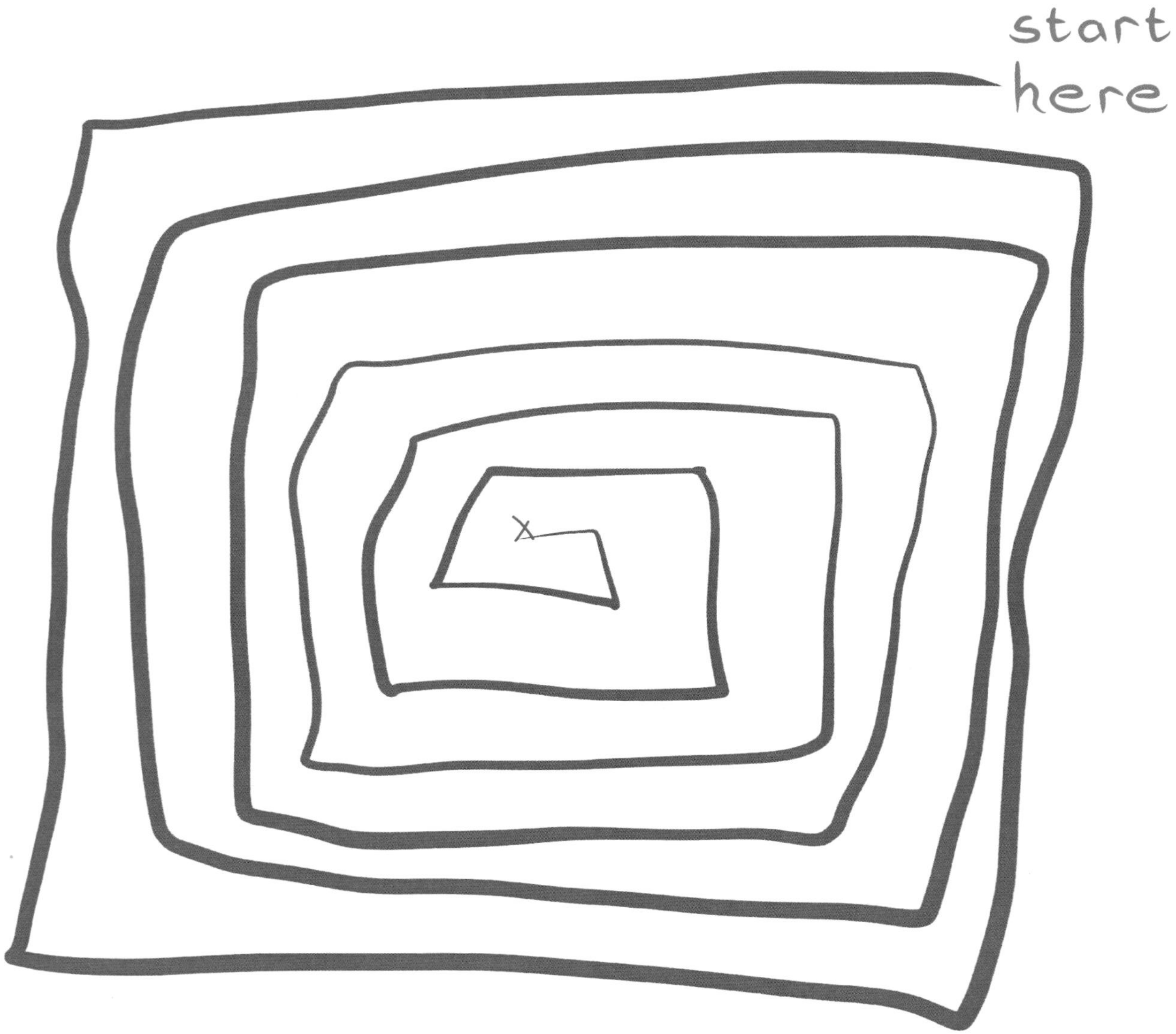
start
here

Press your Thumb

to this page.

Find the **letters** in your name.

Trace them with your finger.

A B C D E F G
H I J K L
M N O P Q
R S T U V W
X Y Z

Now trace your age.

let's take a

DEEP Breath

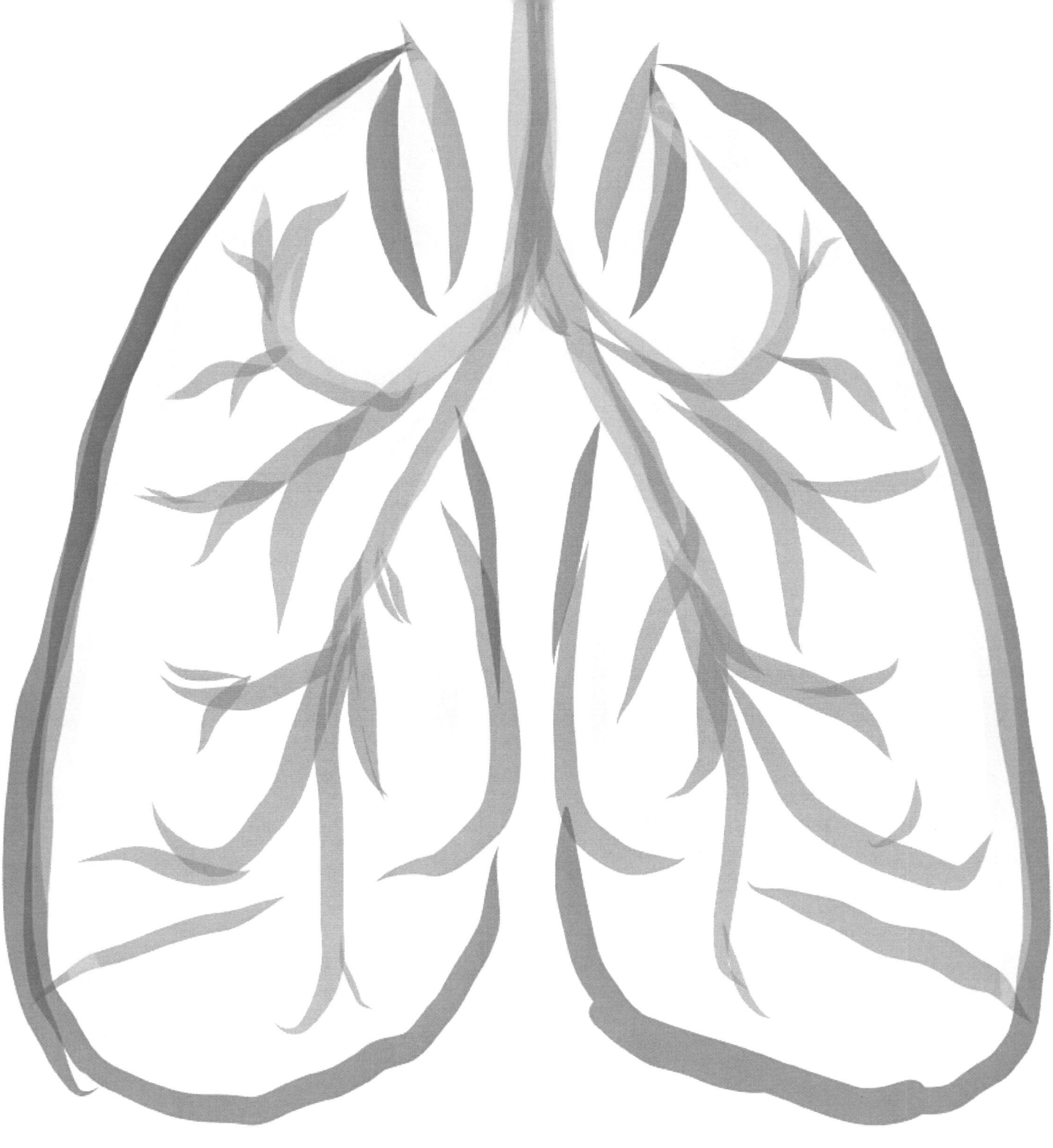

Let

it

GO

Listen

What Can You Hear?

Can you name 3 sounds?

Are they **loud sounds?**

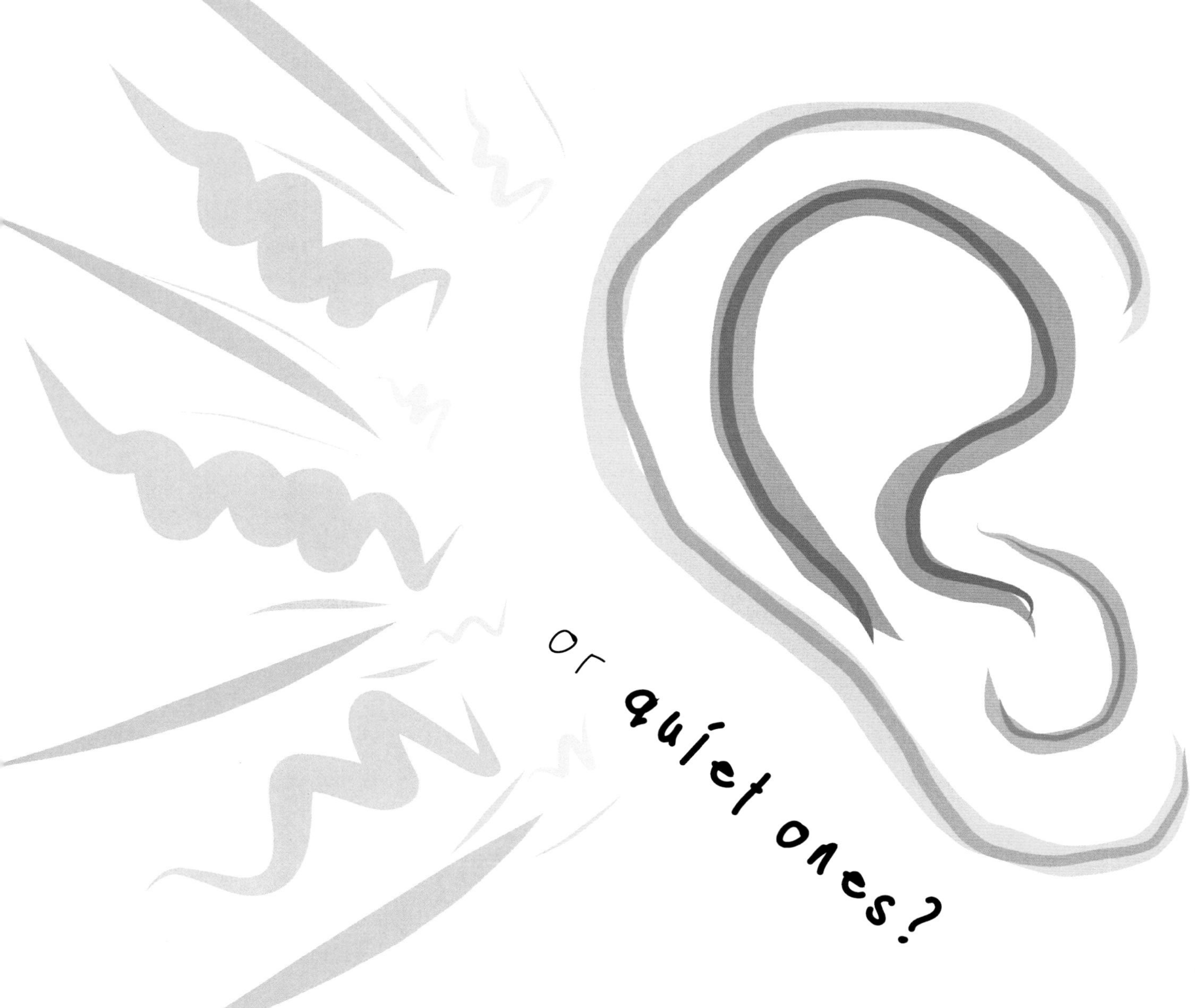

or **quiet ones?**

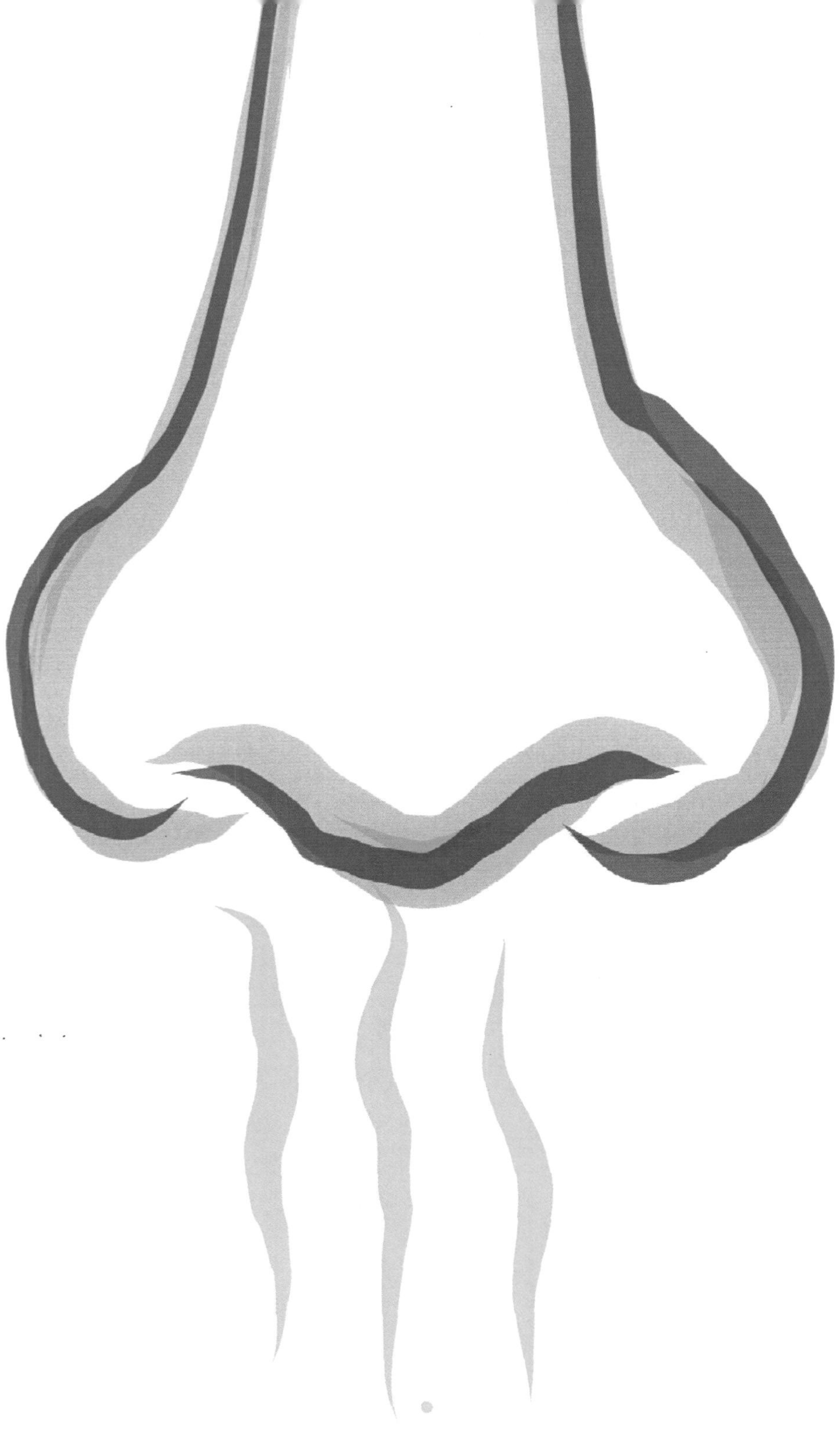

Breathe

in through your nose.

what can you smell?

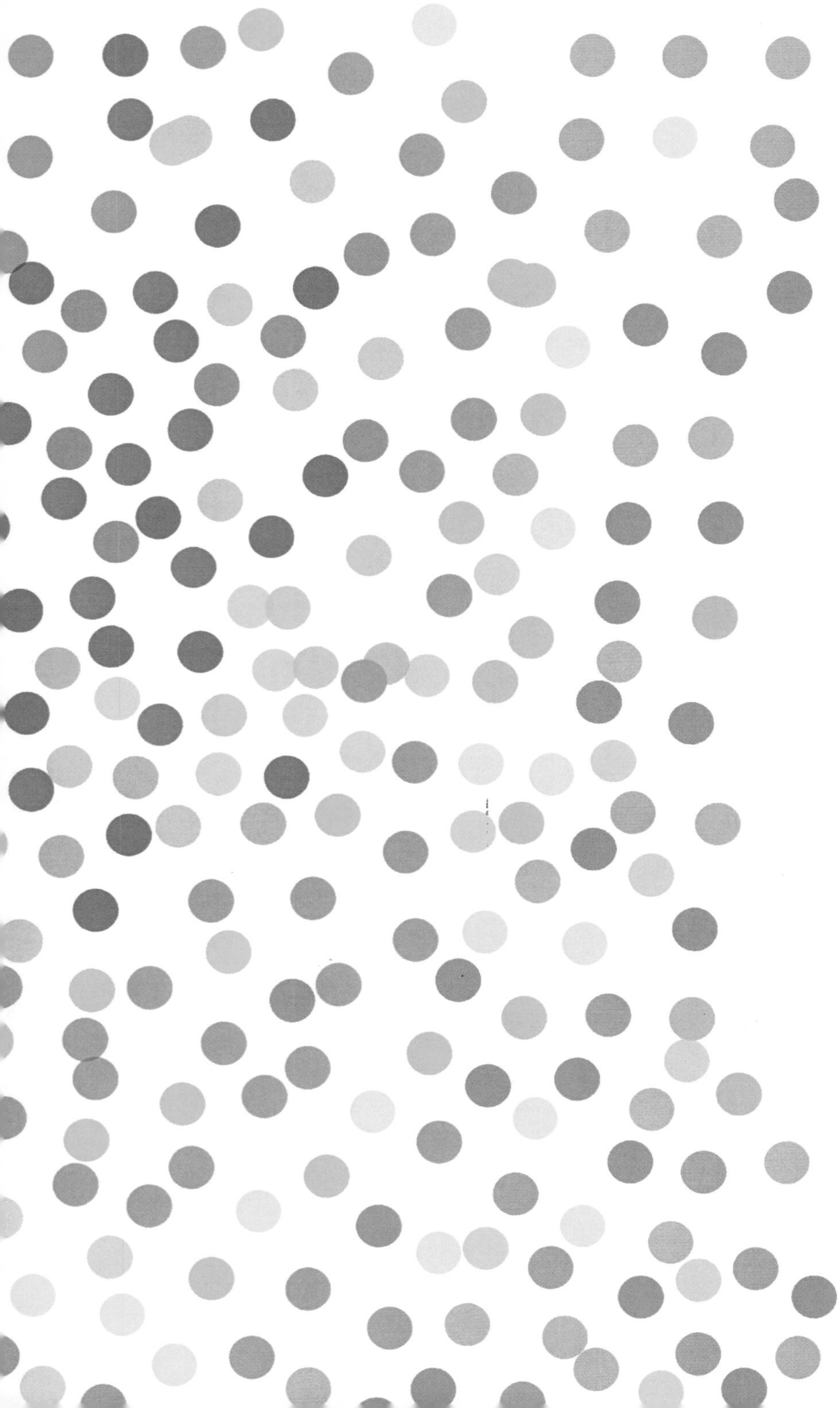

Now smell the book.

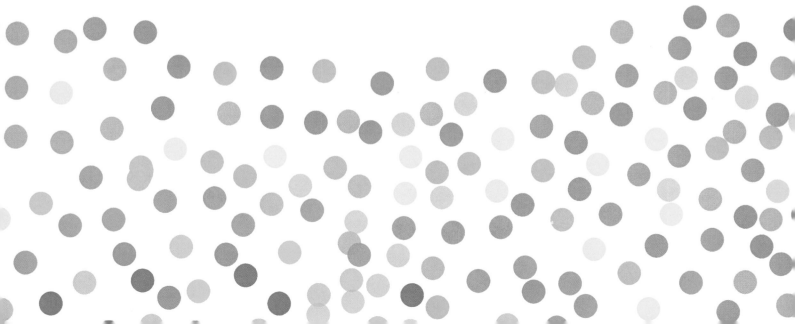

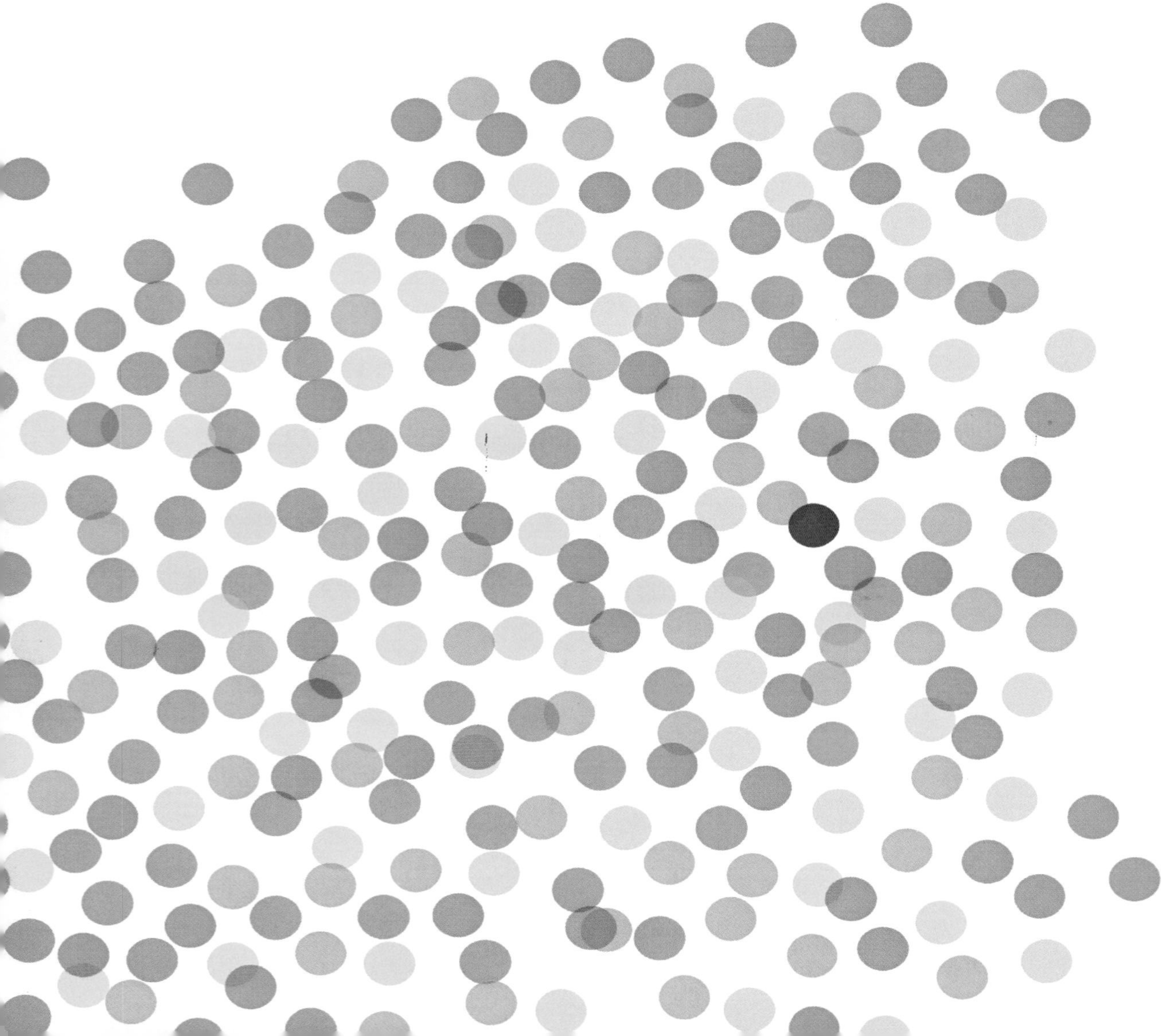

I **DID NOT** expect you to actually do that.

what did it smell like?

Now...

SNIFF your hands.

For real, this time.

SMELL THEM

what do they smell like?

Do you **remember** the last thing you ate?

Can you still taste it on your tongue?

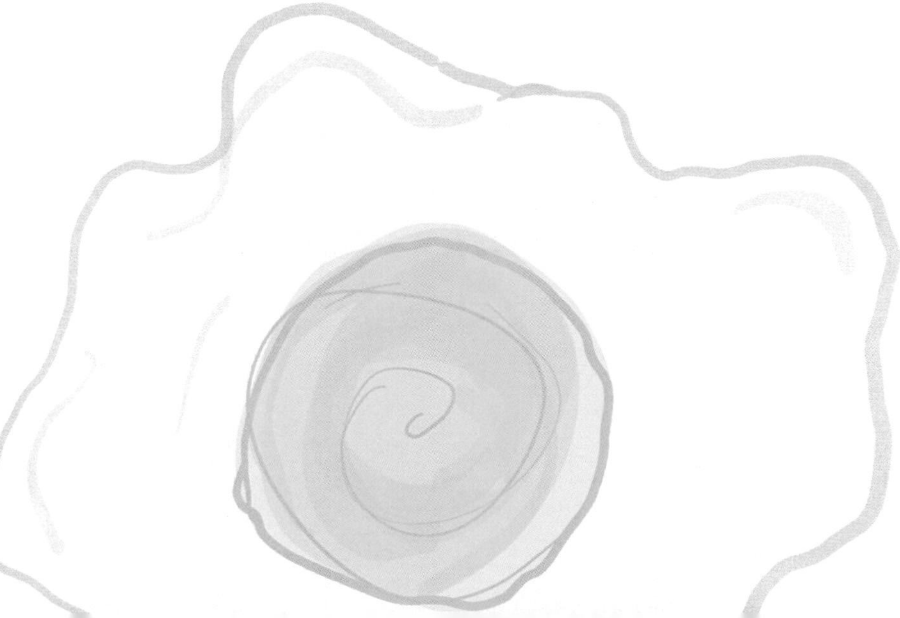

What did it taste like?

Hmm... that's interesting.

Tongues are weird.

Now...

Take
Another
DEEP
BREATH

and...

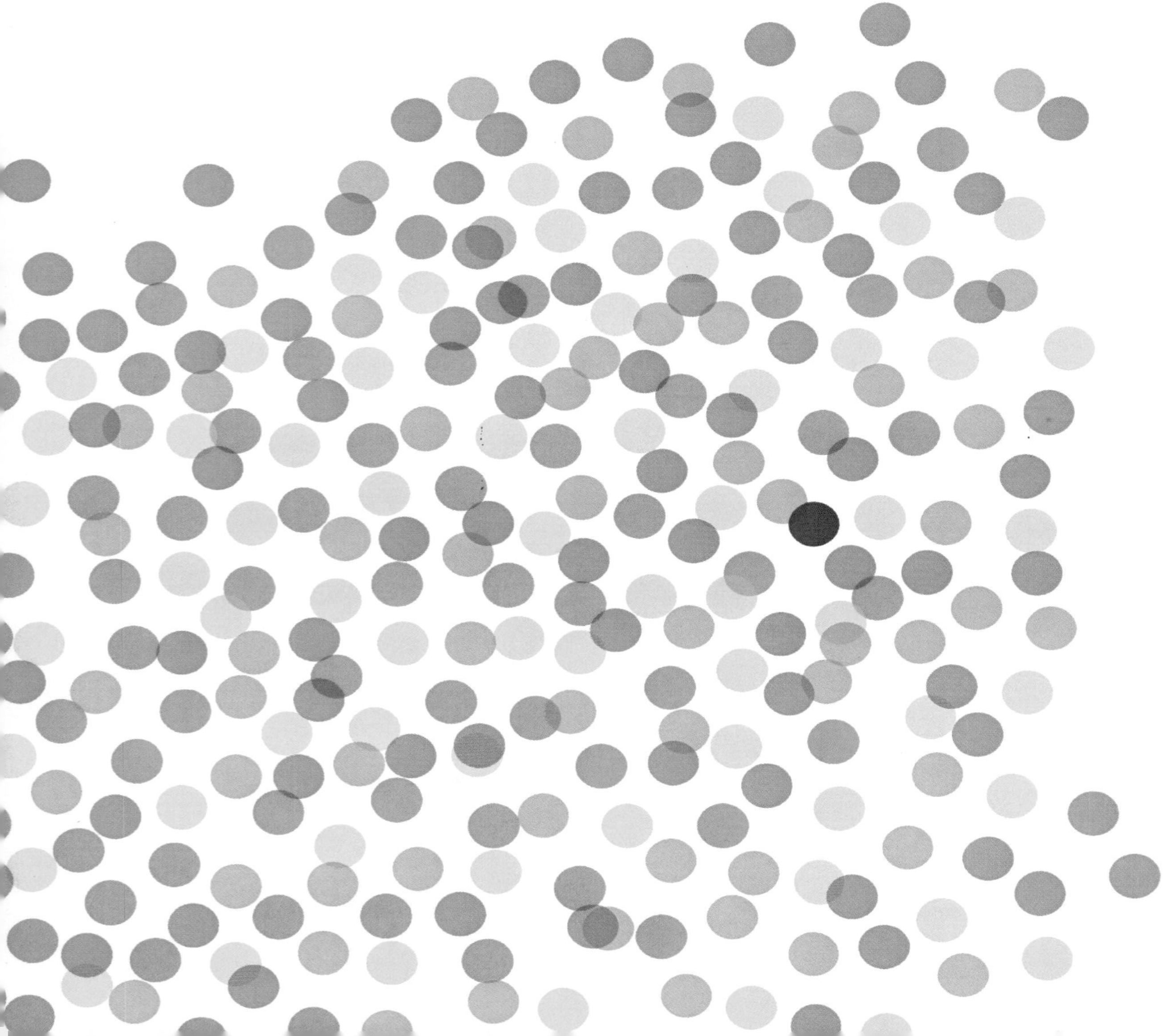

GO!

A Note From The Author

You're probably wondering what all of that was about. I know I would be wondering. We did some weird stuff back there.

Well, it's actually pretty simple.
Sometimes our **brains** need rewiring. They get too **busy** and **mixed up** and they don't quite work right anymore. We get overwhelmed, **worried**, and for whatever reason we just **NEED A BREAK.**

We all get that feeling sometimes.

It's called ANXIETY, and it's really no fun at all.

That's what this book is for.

Taming that big scary ANXIETY feeling.

IN GOD WE TRUST
LIBERTY
ONE CENT
ONE CENT

You may not have noticed, but while you were doing the things in this book, you were rewiring your brain. Each page is designed to help your brain **focus** and **calm down**.

It's called **grounding**, and you can do it without the book, but the book is WAY MORE FUN.

So next time you feel yourself getting too wrapped up in things, and your brain gets all **wibbly wobbly**, and you just aren't yourself...

STOP

and read this book

I hope it helps you.

Your frequently ANXIOUS friend,

Amanda

Psst...

Just so you know, I can't guarantee any of this stuff actually works to calm anxiety or help you regulate emotions. But hopefully it was fun for you anyway.

About the Author

Amanda Silva is a writer, a blogger, and a mom. She is the author of "Nana and Me and the Tree", and the creator of TheBookBadger.Com. She is passionate about mental health and raising strong-minded kids.She lives in Denver, CO with her husband, their son, and a tiny little dog named Sugar.

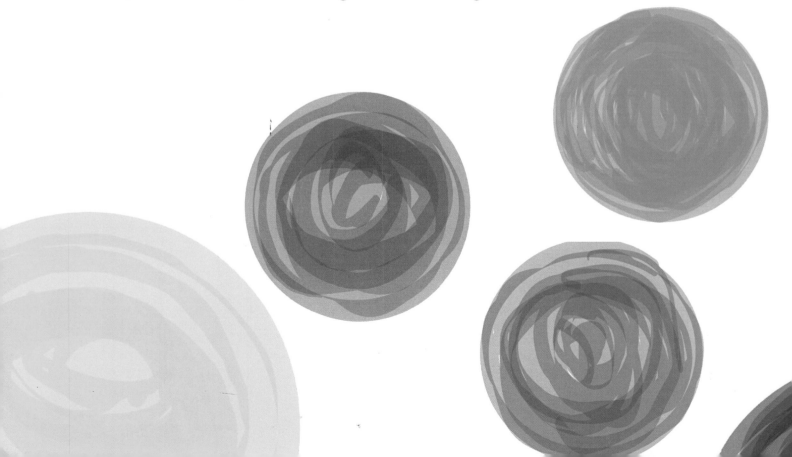

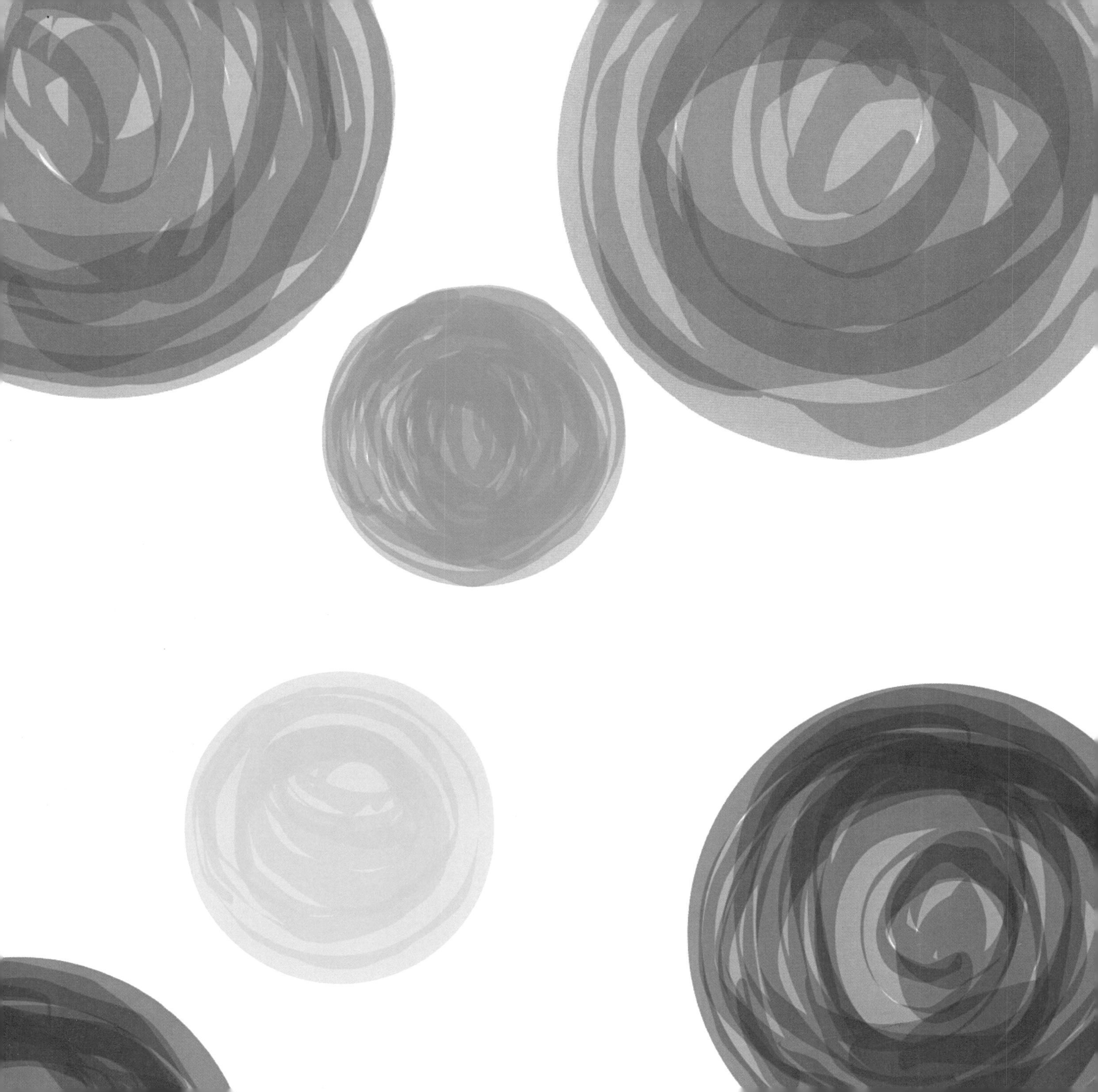

Oh yeah. One last thing.

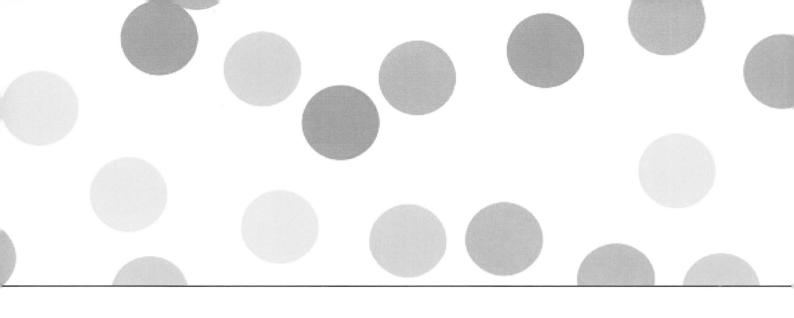

Don't forget to **STOP** and **review** this **book.**

I appreciate it.

Thanks.

www.authoramandasilva.com

Made in United States
North Haven, CT
14 February 2024

48753520R00029